She Persisted

PURA BELPRÉ

―INSPIRED BY―
She Persisted
by Chelsea Clinton & Alexandra Boiger

PURA BELPRÉ

Written by
Meg Medina and Marilisa Jiménez García

Interior illustrations by
Gillian Flint

PHILOMEL

☞ To ☜
all the fearless children's librarians, past and present
—M. M.

☞ For ☜
our Latinx children, families, and storytellers
—M. J. G.

PHILOMEL
An imprint of Penguin Random House LLC, New York

First published in the United States of America by Philomel,
an imprint of Penguin Random House LLC, 2023

Text copyright © 2023 by Chelsea Clinton
Illustrations copyright © 2023 by Alexandra Boiger

Penguin supports copyright. Copyright fuels creativity, encourages diverse voices, promotes free speech, and creates a vibrant culture. Thank you for buying an authorized edition of this book and for complying with copyright laws by not reproducing, scanning, or distributing any part of it in any form without permission. You are supporting writers and allowing Penguin to continue to publish books for every reader.

Philomel is a registered trademark of Penguin Random House LLC.
The Penguin colophon is a registered trademark of Penguin Books Limited.

Visit us online at PenguinRandomHouse.com.

Library of Congress Cataloging-in-Publication Data is available.

HC ISBN 9780593529096
PB ISBN 9780593620618

1st Printing

Printed in the United States of America

LSCC

Edited by Talia Benamy and Jill Santopolo.
Design by Ellice M. Lee.
Text set in LTC Kennerley Pro.

The publisher does not have any control over and does not assume any responsibility for author or third-party websites or their content.

Dear Reader,

As Sally Ride and Marian Wright Edelman both powerfully said, "You can't be what you can't see." When Sally said that, she meant that it was hard to dream of being an astronaut, like she was, or a doctor or an athlete or anything at all if you didn't see someone like you who already had lived that dream. She especially was talking about seeing women in jobs that historically were held by men.

I wrote the first *She Persisted* and the books that came after it because I wanted young girls—and children of all genders—to see women who worked hard to live their dreams. And I wanted all of us to see examples of persistence in the face of different challenges to help inspire us in our own lives.

I'm so thrilled now to partner with a sisterhood of writers to bring longer, more in-depth versions of these stories of women's persistence and achievement to readers. I hope you enjoy these chapter books as much as I do and find them inspiring and empowering.

And remember: If anyone ever tells you no, if anyone ever says your voice isn't important or your dreams are too big, remember these women. They persisted and so should you.

Warmly,
Chelsea Clinton

She Persisted

She Persisted: MARIAN ANDERSON

She Persisted: VIRGINIA APGAR

She Persisted: PURA BELPRÉ

She Persisted: SIMONE BILES

She Persisted: NELLIE BLY

She Persisted: RUBY BRIDGES

She Persisted: KALPANA CHAWLA

She Persisted: CLAUDETTE COLVIN

She Persisted: ELLA FITZGERALD

She Persisted: ROSALIND FRANKLIN

She Persisted: TEMPLE GRANDIN

She Persisted: DEB HAALAND

She Persisted: BETHANY HAMILTON

She Persisted: DOROTHY HEIGHT

She Persisted: FLORENCE GRIFFITH JOYNER

She Persisted: HELEN KELLER

She Persisted: CORETTA SCOTT KING

She Persisted: CLARA LEMLICH

She Persisted: RACHEL LEVINE

She Persisted: MAYA LIN

She Persisted: WANGARI MAATHAI

She Persisted: WILMA MANKILLER

She Persisted: PATSY MINK

She Persisted: FLORENCE NIGHTINGALE

She Persisted: SALLY RIDE

She Persisted: MARGARET CHASE SMITH

She Persisted: SONIA SOTOMAYOR

She Persisted: MARIA TALLCHIEF

She Persisted: DIANA TAURASI

She Persisted: HARRIET TUBMAN

She Persisted: OPRAH WINFREY

She Persisted: MALALA YOUSAFZAI

PURA BELPRÉ

TABLE OF CONTENTS

Chapter 1: *Gather, Children!* 1

Chapter 2: *Growing and Learning in Puerto Rico* 10

Chapter 3: *A New Life in New York* 16

Chapter 4: *Friends, Puppets, and Libraries* ... 25

Chapter 5: *Love for a Storyteller and Author* .. 37

Chapter 6: *Her Storytime Candlelight Burns On* 51

How You Can Persist 58

References 64

CHAPTER 1

Gather, Children!

Gather, children! Sit close and listen, for this is a tale of a girl who told stories about cunning rabbits who defeat tigers, about rainbow-colored horses who bargain for their freedom—even about beautiful cockroaches who fall in love with chivalrous mice. It is a story about a girl named Pura Belpré, who grew up and changed a famous library into a place where everyone could feel welcome.

Although there is some disagreement about the exact date of her birth, Pura Belpre's official birth certificate states that she was born on February 2, 1899, in the tiny mountain town of Cidra, Puerto Rico.

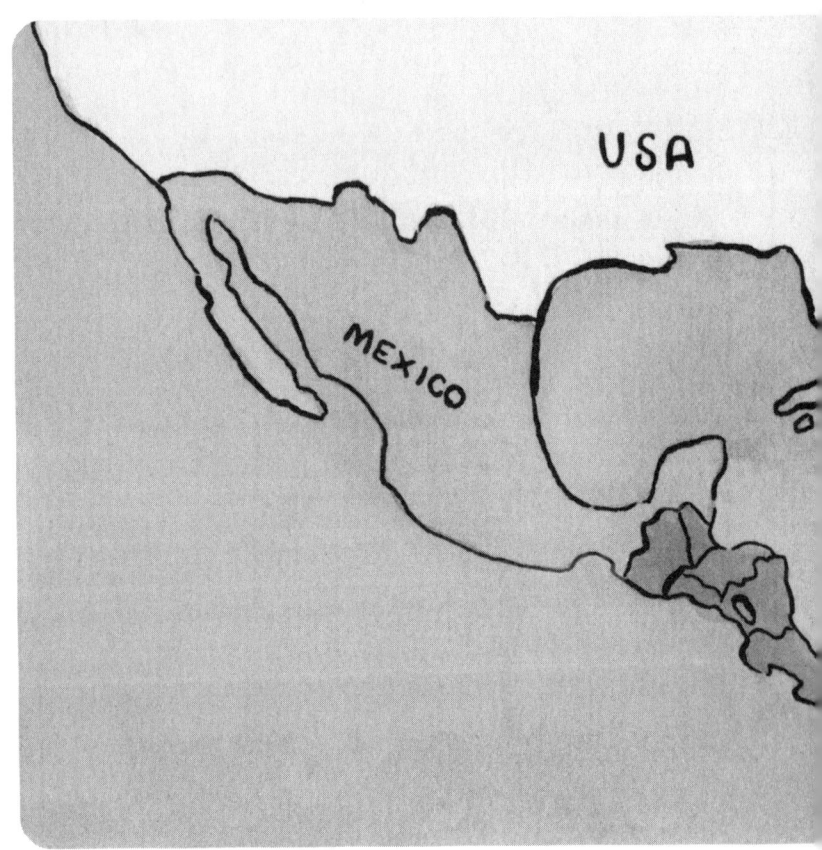

Maybe you have heard of Puerto Rico, or maybe you have even visited. Puerto Rico is a tropical island that sits in the Atlantic Ocean and the Caribbean Sea. Today it is a territory of the United States. But that was not always true.

For more than three hundred years, Puerto Rico was ruled by Spain. But just a few months before Pura Belpré was born, Puerto Rico experienced a very big change. Spain had been fighting against the United States in the Spanish-American War. They were fighting because Spain wanted to keep control of Puerto Rico, along with other territories it ruled, such as Cuba and Guam.

In the end, Spain lost the war. As part of its surrender, Spain signed a document called the Treaty of Paris and agreed to give control of Puerto Rico to the United States. That is how Puerto Rico became a US territory. Puerto Rico is still an unincorporated territory today, which means it has no powers as a state in the US or as its own country. Residents of Puerto Rico cannot vote in US presidential elections. They can't elect their own senators and representatives to the US Congress to vote on laws either. This also means they have no say in who is on the US Supreme Court. There are lots of people who feel that is unfair and would like to change what they believe is Puerto Rico's colonial territory status.

Back then, when the United States took charge, things did not go smoothly. The new government and the Puerto Rican people did not trust or even easily understand each other. New laws were passed that benefitted the US government. Suddenly, people had to pay for things using dollars instead of pesos, which had been the currency until then. Taxes on land were raised, and many people could not afford to keep their farms. All official business had to be done in English instead of Spanish, the language most people had always spoken in their homes and at their jobs. Even school materials were suddenly printed in English. This made it a confusing time of hardship for Puerto Ricans.

To make matters worse, in August of the year Pura was born, one of the most powerful hurricanes in history—Hurricane San Ciriaco—blew across the island and brought twenty-eight days of devastating rain with it. Thousands of people were hurt or killed. Crops were wiped away by the wind, mud, and water. Many towns were destroyed. This left many Puerto Ricans suffering and struggling to find work.

One of those struggling was Pura's father, Felipe. He was a man of possible French descent (no one is entirely sure) who made a living as a construction worker. He moved their family often as he searched for jobs. Pura and her family moved from Cayey, with its pretty mountains and white Spanish-style buildings, to Arroyo, near the Caribbean Sea, where Pura completed first and second grade. After her mother's death and her father's remarriage, the family moved to nearby Guayama, a town where most people worked to produce sugar. All of these moves happened before Pura was in the fifth grade!

In every new home, Pura roamed outside to discover what was around her. Whether in the mountains or near the sea, she was drawn to nature. She loved the bright flamboyán trees, with their red blooms in summer. She listened to the chirping of reina moras, glowing in the trees with their yellow bellies and white-striped heads. She watched rushing rivers and the coquí frogs that lived in the muddy banks nearby.

But even more than she loved nature, Pura loved listening to stories, especially the folktales her grandmother told her aloud from memory. These were stories as old as the mountains. Some stories came from the Taíno Indians, who were the first people to live on the island. Other tales came with people who had arrived later, by choice or by force, from Europe, Africa, and Asia. But they were all stories that were especially popular in Afro Puerto Rican communities such as Pura's, and they had been told and reshaped over time by each storyteller, like her abuela.

So Pura was a girl with three important qualities.

She knew how to face big changes in her life. She had a deep love for her island home of Puerto

Rico. And she had an ear for good stories from all over the world.

Those three things together are how her own exciting story began.

CHAPTER 2

Growing and Learning in Puerto Rico

When Pura's older sister was ready to begin college, Pura's family moved to San Juan, the capital, where the University of Puerto Rico was located.

San Juan was an old colonial city—and a busy one. It had Spanish-style buildings decorated with iron balconies and hidden courtyard gardens. Forts, left over from the days of Spain's rule, still looked out across the bay. One of them was even a prison where inmates, including people who fought for Puerto Rico's independence, were held.

People could get around San Juan for their daily business by an electric tram, nicknamed la jaula, that had stops all around the city. But the best part of San Juan for Pura was that she had cousins who lived there. In the afternoons during siesta time, she would gather them and head to the old forts. Years later she would recall, "With the surf pounding in our ears, we would exchange stories."

A few years later, when Pura graduated from Central High School, she thought she might want to be a teacher, since it offered a path to a college education. She could already speak English, Spanish, and a bit of French. She was interested

in books, current events, and oral stories.

Even though there was a need for teachers, entering college was still unusual for girls in Puerto Rico in 1919, especially for Afro Puerto Rican girls who were not from rich families. It is possible that Pura's father knew important people through his work and political activities who might have helped his daughters gain admission. No one is sure. But whatever the reason, Pura was accepted into the University of Puerto Rico in 1920, ready to learn as much as she could. She was a young woman with a plan for her own future.

But sometimes plans change unexpectedly.

At about that time, Pura received exciting news from far away. A mysterious letter had arrived from a man named Raymond Maduro, who lived in New York. He was asking permission

to marry one of her sisters, Elisa, who had moved to New York to be with another of their sisters, Luisa. Elisa very much wanted her brothers and sisters to attend her wedding.

Of course, Pura decided to go.

What Pura couldn't have guessed, though, is that the short trip for the wedding would open her eyes to an even bigger dream than becoming a teacher. In fact, that trip would change everything about her life.

CHAPTER 3

A New Life in New York

New York City was an exciting place to be in the early 1920s.

When Pura arrived, she found a bustling city of nearly six million people, with ocean steamers entering or leaving the busy port every twenty minutes. There were banks and businesses and thousands of factories that produced everything from women's coats and hats to cigar boxes, coffins, and rubber tires. Workers came to fill all those jobs. Many African Americans migrated to New York City from the South, looking for new opportunities. Other people arrived as immigrants from Europe or the West Indies, crossing oceans to start their new lives in the United States. It was also the time of the first large migration of Puerto Ricans, who had been facing a lack of job opportunities on their island. In addition to coming for the lure of jobs, they came to New York as United States citizens, a right that had been recently granted by President Woodrow Wilson.

As more and more people moved to New York City, neighborhoods grew and changed.

Like her sisters Luisa and Elisa, Pura enjoyed the energy of Nueva York, so she decided to stay with Elisa after the wedding. To help with

expenses, she took a job at the William Morris Company on West 22nd Street, near the Garment District. The company made petticoats, slips, and bathing suits and was one of eight thousand women's wear factories in the city at that time.

But a much better opportunity arrived very soon after.

Elisa and Raymond had many interesting friends who visited their apartment. Among them was a professor of Spanish named Mr. Colón. During one of his visits, Mr. Colón mentioned that he had a librarian friend who was looking for an assistant.

"The neighborhood uptown has many new bodegas and barbershops, and my friend wants someone who can speak Spanish. I think Elisa is exactly who she needs!" said Mr. Colón.

Raymond did not like that idea at all. Like many men of his time, he did not believe a married woman should work outside her home.

"I'm sorry," he said, "but my wife is not going to work."

Elisa, who was listening carefully, spoke up right away. "Why doesn't Pura apply instead?"

And so it was agreed that Pura would interview for the job.

Mr. Colón introduced Pura to Miss Ernestine Rose, who was the newly appointed library supervisor of the 135th Street branch in Harlem. Ernestine was a white Jewish woman who believed that the neighborhood around her library would soon become mostly Spanish-speaking. She was interested in hiring more Black and Spanish-speaking librarians. Her bosses wanted her to

develop exciting and vibrant materials for the community. Would Pura like to be part of that effort?

Excited for the challenge, Pura said yes.

Pura didn't know it yet, but she had come into the library system at one of its most exciting times in history.

Beautiful libraries had been getting built all over the city because members of wealthy New York families chose to become philanthropists. A philanthropist is a person who donates money to help people out in any number of ways, including by building things for an entire community to enjoy. One of the most well-known New York philanthropists was Andrew Carnegie, who added his money to the donations of the Astor, Lenox, and Tilden family foundations to build sixty-five public libraries all over the city. These donations made other exciting developments possible, too. They helped establish a new collection of Black history, literature, and culture that was being organized by a man named Arturo Schomburg, an Afro Puerto Rican scholar in the New York Public Library system. The money was also being used to improve the collection of materials for a particular group of people who hadn't been served very well by the library until then.

Children, just like you, were now being welcomed at the library.

CHAPTER 4
....

Friends, Puppets, and Libraries

Today we think of libraries as welcoming places for children, with many colorful shelves of books, fun maker spaces, comfortable chairs, and lots of exciting programs to choose from.

But that was not always the case.

Long ago, libraries were not very kid-friendly, and children under fourteen were simply not allowed in. Library directors believed that children were loud and unruly, and that they couldn't be trusted to treat books gently. But one person felt differently.

Anne Carroll Moore was the first public library administrator in charge of growing services for children in the New York Public Library. For years she had been arguing that children deserved to be at the library. Anne hired the first children's librarians. She wanted diverse and energetic librarians and assistants who were creative and who knew many languages. She wanted them to have information about stories from around the world, and she didn't care very much if they had college degrees. What mattered most was getting the best books for children.

This was the perfect job for Pura! So, in 1921, she became an assistant at the 135th Street branch, later known as the Countee Cullen Library.

The library was located right in the heart of Harlem, which was a thriving African American community that was home to Caribbean immigrants, including Afro-Caribbean communities, too. Pura was excited to meet colleagues like Arturo Schomburg, whose collection of materials specifically on Black culture would also include the Spanish-speaking world.

As an assistant, Pura had many duties, such as shelving books, checking out materials, and running story time. One of Pura's duties was also to read all the books on the fairy-tale shelves. Why? Anne had asked for books and stories that reflected the children in the community. Pura could see there was a growing number of Puerto Rican children in Harlem, so she looked high and low on those shelves for international folktales

like the ones she had always heard as a child. Imagine her shock when she found none!

How could she help solve that problem? She began doing research into Puerto Rican folktales and making recommendations. And she also persisted by writing down the stories she had heard from her grandmother. When it was her turn to run story time, she told those stories. Soon people noticed that she was an excellent storyteller.

Each time she began the story hour, she would light a wishing candle so the children could listen to the story by candlelight. Her voice was deep and calm. She looked at each child as she spoke. She used hand gestures and created different voices for the characters. When the story was done, the children would make a wish and blow out the candle together. Other famous authors and storytellers who visited the library agreed that Pura created an experience that transported the children through their imagination. Her much-admired colleague Arturo even urged her to write the stories down for children.

Soon, her bosses and colleagues noticed, too, and they encouraged Pura to become a full-time librarian herself. So she enrolled in New York Public Library School. One of her classes was taught by Mary Gould Davis, who was supervisor of storytelling for the entire library system. Mary especially loved folktales, and she encouraged her students at library school to pick unusual tales that children might not find on their own.

Pura knew just the right story to present for her first class assignment. She remembered a story she'd learned from her grandmother. It was "Pérez and Martina," about a beautiful cockroach named Martina and a gallant little mouse named Pérez who falls in love with her. She wrote the story down and told it in class exactly as her grandmother had told it to her—even with a slightly scary ending of Pérez dying in a boiling pot. The story was so well received that Pura was invited to present it to other librarians at the annual library symposium. (A symposium is a special meeting where people gather to discuss a particular topic.) *Pérez and Martina* would prove to be so popular that it was published as a book a few years later by the Frederick Warne Company. Pura's favorite story had become the first Latino storybook published by a major publisher in the United States.

Pura worked at many branches of the library and with many different immigrant groups. By the time she was transferred to the 115th Street branch, she had built up a large collection of stories, which was very useful. The neighborhood had once been heavily Jewish, but now many Puerto

Rican families lived there. An old synagogue had become a church called La Milagrosa. It was the first Spanish-language church of the Puerto Rican community. The church offered children's programs in Spanish for interested mothers. One day, Pura saw a puppet show performed there by the young brother of one of the librarians. Pura remembered that as a child she had enjoyed puppets. She had made doll figures using long mangoes, on which she'd draw faces and add hair. She decided she would use puppets at her library branch.

Slowly, the branch became a true center for the community. Pura worked tirelessly to offer what the community wanted and needed. There were lots of programs for adults, such as art exhibits and lectures, but also exciting programs for children, including events that had never been done before. The library was the first branch to celebrate el Día de Reyes—Three Kings Day—in early January, which is when children in Puerto Rico and other countries receive their Christmas presents. And best of all, they began to offer puppet-making classes and puppet shows performed by the neighborhood children. These shows were immediately popular. Even on snowy days, families came to enjoy the performances, especially since they were based on stories they remembered from Puerto Rico. Soon, Pura was being asked to bring the puppet shows to other branches and community centers all over the city.

As the years went by, Pura's reputation as a masterful librarian, puppeteer, and storyteller grew, no matter which branch she worked in. If there was conflict in a community, such as East Harlem, she used stories to help children of different backgrounds come together. At the Aguilar branch, she designed a club called the Little Women's Club to encourage even the strictest parents to allow their daughters to spend time at the library with friends. She taught boys how to make marionette-style puppets. By 1940, she was so successful there that she was invited to a national librarian conference in Cincinnati, Ohio, to present her ideas for how best to work with Spanish-speaking patrons. Librarians from all over the country would be listening to her ideas.

Pura eagerly headed to Ohio.

It was in Cincinnati, however, that Pura would meet someone who would change her life yet again.

CHAPTER 5

Love for a Storyteller and Author

Pura was a success at the librarians' conference. Handsomely dressed, she took the stage and held her audience's attention as she explained her ideas in her steady, rich voice. Afterward, Pura chatted about her book, *Pérez and Martina*, with a gentleman who was in the audience. The two promised to stay in touch.

That man was Clarence Cameron White, a famous African American musician and conductor.

He was an elegant older gentleman with wire-rimmed glasses and neat tweed suits. His music was often based on Black history and folklore. For example, he had won a very important award for writing an opera based on the life of Jean-Jacques Dessalines, the formerly enslaved man who led his people in revolt against the French and later became the Emperor of Haiti.

Not long after meeting Pura, Clarence's wife, Beatrice, died, and he became a widower.

Pura and Clarence soon fell in love, writing each other many letters. They married in 1943 and moved into a studio apartment in Harlem's sophisticated Sugar Hill neighborhood. At first, Pura was unsure she wanted to leave her mostly Puerto Rican neighborhood in East Harlem, but she soon grew to appreciate her exciting new

community. Their building on Edgecombe Avenue was the tallest and most desired apartment house in Harlem at the time, and it attracted many famous writers, musicians, intellectuals, and community activists as tenants. The famous painter

Aaron Douglas, social leader W. E. B. Du Bois, and Thurgood Marshall, who would go on to become a Supreme Court justice, all made their home in that building. The neighbors often attended parties together to have conversations about Black excellence and other important matters of the time.

But married life was going to take many more adjustments than just deciding where to live. A bigger decision for Pura was whether to remain a librarian. She loved her work, but her new husband's career required a lot of travel to many cities for rehearsals and performances. Being apart was difficult for the new couple, but leaving the work she loved seemed painful, too. They wrote back and forth often to consider the question of what to do.

Finally, Pura and Clarence made their decision. Pura asked for a one-year leave of absence from the library. During that break, she would travel with her husband but also write and perform stories of her own. However, her time away from the library ended up being much longer than twelve months. In fact, it stretched to nearly twenty years! While Clarence worked on his performances, Pura continued her storytelling in the cities where they traveled. She often used the same handful of stories that included magic, animals, and country life from Puerto Rico. All of them were stories that children might not find on their own, and they all had both funny parts and scary parts she knew children would enjoy. In 1946, she published them as her second book, *The Tiger and the Rabbit and Other Stories*, which was the first English collection of Puerto Rican folktales published in the United States.

For many years after that, Pura did not publish another book, although she persisted in writing. During the summers, while Clarence participated in an annual music festival in Tanglewood, Massachusetts, Pura kept herself busy working on an idea for a shorter story about a country boy character called Juan Bobo. She also tried writing a whole novel about a girl named Teresa who was very similar to herself. In the novel, Teresa returns to her rural plantation home in between Cidra and Cayey to discover a mystery about her brother. Unfortunately, Pura could not find a publisher who was interested at the time.

Her difficulties with publishing were not the only sad experience for Pura. Clarence was much older than Pura, by about twenty years. When he died of cancer in 1960, it seemed to Pura that her whole world had changed again—but this time for the worse.

Pura's friends at the library soon came to her with an idea. Why not come back to the library? They created a position for her: Spanish Children's Specialist. Before long, she was busier than ever. She went to schools, libraries, and story hours in all five boroughs of New York City. She bought quality materials for libraries and had the chance, once again, to meet children and their families—now including some from many different countries across the Caribbean and Latin America. So, while it was a sad personal time for Pura, she found a way to change that sadness into something positive. She found it rewarding to "be greeted by a group of children who still remember the stories you told, to have a child ask you to repeat a story he missed because his friend told him it was 'super,' to overhear a Jewish boy plead with his mother to let him stay for the story hour just this once."

Then Pura was asked to work on a very special project. The South Bronx had a very large population of people from Puerto Rico, the Dominican Republic, Cuba, and other countries where political and economic problems had caused them to leave their homes and move to New York. The South Bronx community needed better education and recreation services for families who spoke Spanish. According to Lillian López, the young librarian who was organizing it, the goal of the South Bronx Library Project was to "break down barriers between the library and the community." Lillian was also Puerto Rican, and she came from a family that believed strongly in education and justice. In fact, her sister Evelina López Antonetty was a well-known community leader who had founded United Bronx Parents, an organization that supported bilingual education and free food services, among other school improvements.

Lillian and Pura were soon working together with other Puerto Rican leaders to help strengthen public schools and build the community. For the first time, schools were teaching in bilingual formats to help students who spoke languages other than English at home—and Pura knew a lot about how to do that well. Lillian created lists of books for teachers to use. Pura brought bilingual

presentations and stories to her school and daycare visits. She was so successful that, in 1973, school district 16 even named their traveling bookmobile the Pura Belpré Children's Caravan. The bus went from school to school. It had red carpeting and projection screens. There were books to borrow and art easels so children could draw pictures about the books and stories they read. Pura also ran a new storytelling and puppetry program at El Museo del Barrio, and she designed story programs for adults, too. Even ladies who worked as seamstresses in a factory could count on having Pura come to tell them a story.

On top of all that, Pura wrote more than ever during this busy time. Her persistence over the years had paid off, and now publishers were paying attention. She was sixty-three years old when she finally published the story she had begun during the summers at Tanglewood with Clarence. It was called *Juan Bobo and the Queen's Necklace*. Two years later, her librarian friend Augusta Baker convinced the Lippincott Company to publish a new edition of *The Tiger and the Rabbit and Other Tales* with more stories added and new illustrations. Pura recorded *Pérez and Martina* as an LP, which was an early form of audio recording.

A few years later, she published two more books. *Oté*, a Puerto Rican folktale about outwitting a devilish trickster, and *Santiago*, an award-winning book about the friendships between a Puerto Rican boy in New York and his classmates. She revised one of the stories from *The Tiger and the Rabbit* into its own book called *The Dance of Animals*. She wrote a collection of tales called *Once in Puerto Rico* about the original Taíno people of Puerto Rico and Spanish settlers. She was almost eighty years old when she published *The Rainbow-Colored Horse* about a seven-color horse that bargains for his freedom with the boy who captures him. She also wrote several unpublished stories, too, such as "Inés" and "Mariita," stories about strong girls who used their wits and magic to solve their problems. And, of course, she wrote many speeches and essays.

Everywhere she went, people recognized Pura Belpré as an elegant older woman whom they had always known as a respected storyteller and a librarian. Now, though, they knew her as an accomplished author and a wise social leader, too.

CHAPTER 6

Her Storytime Candlelight Burns On

As Pura advanced in age, people often hosted tribute dinners to her or requested interviews to hear her wisdom on how best to work with communities.

That was especially true in 1982. In May of that year, Pura received a very special invitation. She was asked to come to Gracie Mansion, the home of New York City's then-mayor, Edward Koch. She was to receive the Mayor's Award of

Honor for Arts and Culture. She received the honor for improving the cultural life of New Yorkers through her work with public libraries and community centers. The speakers that night

called her a quiet pioneer who enriched the lives of all children.

The following month, Pura received another special award, this time from her Puerto Rican community. A few years earlier, Boricua College had been established in New York City as the only private Latino college on the US mainland. On June 25, the college honored Pura for her lifetime contributions to the Puerto Rican community.

Only a week later, on July 1, 1982, Pura died peacefully in her sleep. She was eighty-three years old.

When someone dies, those who knew them often find comfort by reflecting on that person's life. They remember and appreciate all the special things the person contributed while they were alive. That is what happened after Pura died.

In October of that year, the American Library Association (ALA) wrote to Pura's sister Elisa to say that the organization had passed a resolution to honor Pura. Margaret Mary Kimmel, president of the Association of Library Services for Children, a part of ALA, wrote: "Her many contributions to our profession and her consistent enthusiasm in sharing her rich heritage and love for Puerto Rican children everywhere will keep her in our minds and hearts." In 1996, the American Library Association went even further by establishing the Pura Belpré Award. The award is presented each year to Latino/Latina children's book authors and illustrators "whose work best portrays, affirms, and celebrates the Latino cultural experience in an outstanding work of literature for children and youth." Every

author who wins that award becomes part of Pura's dream for books and stories from all over the Spanish-speaking world.

That same year, to help keep some of Pura's work in print, Arte Público Press published *Firefly Summer*, a novel that Pura wrote during World

War II and was unable to publish in her lifetime.

People have continued to honor Pura's legacy in recent years, too. In 2022, the corner of East 109th Street and Lexington Avenue in East Harlem was renamed Pura Belpré Way.

Most importantly, though, Pura's ideas and vision live on in many people. She began her work as a librarian almost one hundred years ago, and many of the things Pura believed in and fought for then are embraced by librarians today. When you see materials at the library offered in Spanish and other languages, you can thank Pura for her efforts to find books that told everyone's story, especially those of Puerto Rican children. When you attend an exciting children's program at your library, you can thank the early librarians, like Pura, who knew that children, like you, should always find events to engage their imaginations at the library. And if you are a Latino/Latina child—maybe one who has had to learn English or who is new to a community—remember that you have heroes like Pura, who knew you would be coming and who used her persistence to pave the way for you.

HOW YOU CAN PERSIST

by Meg Medina and Marilisa Jiménez García

Do you love books, stories, and communities? You can use that love to honor Pura's legacy, too.

1. Read books that win the Pura Belpré medal. You can ask your librarian to order books from the Pura Belpré list. You can find past winners listed here:

ALA.org/ALSC/AwardsGrants/BookMedia/Belpre

2. Create puppets and perform your favorite story for friends or family. You can use socks, Popsicle sticks, paper bags, and many other materials to make characters that can tell a story.

3. Volunteer as a student assistant at your school or local public library. You can get community service points for your school and be surrounded by great books to read.

4. Write down favorite stories you were told in your family. You can use software that is free or nearly free to turn one of them into a book.

5. Enjoy audiobooks of folktales from

all over the world. You can listen and imagine the characters yourself!

6. Read some of Pura's work at the library. Although most of Pura's books are now out of print, you can still find *Firefly Summer*, *Pérez and Martina*, and many other books at the library. Ask a trusted librarian to help you check them out or order them for the collection.

7. Study and learn about the countries and territories in the Caribbean and about Afro Latinos. Pura believed that Caribbean people had a wealth of stories and history to offer the world. Here is a good place to start: Anansesem.com.

The Use of Terms in This Book

You will notice that in this book, we used different terms to describe Pura and the important people in her life.

In the United States, we sometimes hear the terms Black and African American used to mean the same thing. But not everyone uses them that way today, and we felt it was not the best way to describe Pura and the people in her community. Long ago, European slave traders took Black people from their homelands throughout the world and brought them against their will to other countries. All of those people are Black, and Blackness is an experience and identity that now exists in countries and communities all over the world. The term African American specifically describes Blackness in communities that grew in the US.

Throughout our book, then, when we were discussing people, events, and ideas that had to do with Black cultures worldwide, we used the term Black. When we were talking about Black culture that was very specifically about the US, we used African American.

You will also notice that we have used the terms

Latina and Latino in the book, as well as the term Afro Puerto Rican.

Describing the many people in our country whose roots descend from Spain or its former colonies throughout Latin America and the Caribbean has been very difficult over the years. Terms have included: Spanish, Hispanic, Latina/o, Latinx, or more recently Latine. The trouble has been that no single word can describe more than twenty different countries, each with their own histories, languages, and people.

Our preference was to be specific whenever possible. So, to honor Pura's heritage as a Black woman from Puerto Rico, we referred to her as an Afro Puerto Rican woman. On two occasions, we used Latino and Latina to mean children from many possible backgrounds in Latin America and the Caribbean.

Acknowledgments

We'd like to extend a big thanks to Chelsea Clinton for inviting us to write about this fascinating librarian. It was a dream come true to be part of the Persisterhood and to have Pura Belpré honored in this way.

A big shout-out to the librarians and staff at the Center for Puerto Rican Studies at Hunter College, where the Pura Belpré archives are housed. (These are all of Pura's writings, speeches, photographs, letters, and important documents.) The collection was a treasure chest of information, and the staff made researching there an utter pleasure.

Meg would also like to thank the librarians at New York Public Library for helping her fact-check hard-to-find information, especially regarding the last months of Pura Belpré's life.

Marilisa would like to thank her parents, Carlos and Carmen Jiménez, for developing her love of her bilingual culture and for encouraging her to become a writer.

Finally, we both want to thank each other for the chance to work together. It was an honor to use our shared talents and expertise to ensure Pura's incredible life and contributions received the respect and nuance they have always deserved.

References

Aguilar, Eduardo. *Pura Belpré: Storyteller.* A Center for Puerto Rican Studies Video Production, Hunter College, CUNY.

Association for Library Services to Children, a division of the American Library Association. "Pura Belpré Award." ala.org/alsc/awardsgrants/bookmedia/belpre.

CBC Radio. "Why Goodnight Moon Didn't Make New York Public Library's List of Most Checked-Out Books." *As It Happens*, January 15, 2020. cbc.ca/radio/asithappens/as-it-happens-tuesday-edition-1.5426388/why-goodnight-moon-didn-t-make-new-york-public-library-s-list-of-most-checked-out-books-1.5428049.

Center for Puerto Rican Studies Library & Archives. "Arnold Hyman Profile on Pura Belpré, 1970." Personal and Biographical Information. Articles about Pura Belpré 1932–1979. Pura Belpré Papers, 1897–1985. Center for Puerto Rican Studies, Hunter College, CUNY. Box 1, folder 3.

Center for Puerto Rican Studies Library & Archives. "Bilingual Storyteller." Other Writings, 1960–1969. Pura Belpré Papers, 1897–1985. Center for Puerto Rican Studies, Hunter College, CUNY. Box 19, folder 4.

Center for Puerto Rican Studies Library & Archives. "Birth Certificate" and "Graduation Program." Personal and Biographical Information 1931–1985. Pura Belpré Papers, 1897–1985. Center for Puerto Rican Studies, Hunter College, CUNY. Box 2, folder 4.

Center for Puerto Rican Studies Library & Archives. "Correspondence to Mrs. Raymond Maduro from the American Library Association." Lillian López Papers, 1928–2005. Center for Puerto Rican Studies, Hunter College, CUNY. Box 3, folder 12, page 1.

Center for Puerto Rican Studies Library & Archives. "Exhibition Panels." Graphic Materials. Pura Belpré Papers, 1897–1985. Center for Puerto Rican Studies, Hunter College, CUNY. Box OS III.

Center for Puerto Rican Studies Library & Archives. "Folktales." Writings, 1932–1989. Pura Belpré Papers, 1897–1985. Center for Puerto Rican Studies, Hunter College, CUNY. Box 13–18.

Center for Puerto Rican Studies Library & Archives. "Guide to the Lillian López Papers 1928–2005 (Bulk 1970–1980)." Lillian López Papers, 1928–2005. Center for Puerto Rican Studies, Hunter College, CUNY. centroarchives.hunter.cuny.edu/repositories/2/resources/26.

Center for Puerto Rican Studies Library & Archives. "Interview with Pura Belpré on April 4, 1976." Lillian

López Papers, 1928–2005. Center for Puerto Rican Studies, Hunter College, CUNY. Tape 1, Side A: LiLo. PBel.04.04.1976.b07.1a.

Center for Puerto Rican Studies Library & Archives. "Letter to Clarence White." Correspondence. Pura Belpré Papers, 1897–1985. Center for Puerto Rican Studies, Hunter College, CUNY. Box 12, folder 1.

Center for Puerto Rican Studies Library & Archives. "Mixed Materials." Personal and Biographical Information 1931–1985. Pura Belpré Papers, 1897–1985. Center for Puerto Rican Studies, Hunter College, CUNY. Box 1, folder 8.

Center for Puerto Rican Studies Library & Archives. "New York City Mayor's Awards." Tributes/Mixed Materials. Pura Belpré Papers, 1897–1985. Center for Puerto Rican Studies, Hunter College, CUNY. Box 2, folder 8.

Center for Puerto Rican Studies Library & Archives. Photographs 1929–1969. Pura Belpré Papers, 1897–1985. Center for Puerto Rican Studies, Hunter College, CUNY. Box 29–33.

Center for Puerto Rican Studies Library & Archives. Pura Belpré and Clarence Cameron White 1940–1949. Pura Belpré Papers, 1897–1985. Center for Puerto Rican Studies, Hunter College, CUNY. Box 30.

Center for Puerto Rican Studies Library & Archives. Pura Belpré with Family and Friends 1920–1929. Pura Belpré

Papers, 1897–1985. Center for Puerto Rican Studies, Hunter College, CUNY. Box 30.

"The Connected City." National Museum of American History. May 9, 2019. americanhistory.si.edu/america-on-the-move/connected-city.

de la Vega, Caridad, James A. Jacobs, and Arleen Pabón-Charneco. "National Historic Landmark Nomination: Old San Juan Historic District." United States Department of the Interior, National Park Service. June 1, 2012, npshistory.com/publications/nr-forms/pr/old-san-juan.pdf.

González, Lisa Sánchez. *The Stories I Read to the Children: The Life and Writing of Pura Belpré, the Legendary Storyteller, Children's Author, and New York Public Librarian.* New York: Centro Press, 2013.

Gray, Christopher. "Streetscapes/409 Edgecombe Avenue; An Address That Drew the City's Black Elite." *The New York Times*, July 24, 1994. nytimes.com/1994/07/24/realestate/streetscapes-409-edgecombe-avenue-an-address-that-drew-the-city-s-black-elite.html.

Jiménez García, Marilisa. "Pura Belpré Lights the Storyteller's Candle: Reframing the Legacy of a Legend and What it Means for the Fields of Latino/a Studies and Children's Literature." *Centro Journal*. Center for Puerto Rican Studies, Hunter College, CUNY. Volume XXVI, no. 1 (Spring 2014): 110–145.

Jiménez García, Marilisa, *Side by Side: US Empire, Puerto Rico, and the Roots of American Youth Literature and Culture.* Jackson, MS: The University Press of Mississippi, 2021.

Klepper, Rachel "United Bronx Parents—A 'Community Grown Organization.'" Columbia Rare Book & Manuscript Library, Columbia University. July 18, 2019. blogs.cul.columbia.edu/rbml/2019/07/18/united-bronx-parents-a-community-grown-organization.

Korrol, Virginia E. Sánchez. *From Colonia to Community: The History of Puerto Ricans in New York City.* Berkeley and Los Angeles: University of California Press, 1994.

"Landmark Preservation Commission, LP 1861: '409 Edgecombe Avenue Borough of Manhattan.'" Summary report of meeting, New York, New York, June 15, 1993.

Lareau, Louise. "NYPL's Anne Carroll Moore: A Pioneer Who Opened Library Doors to Kids . . . Literally." *New York Public Library Blog*, March 8, 2021. nypl.org/blog/2021/03/08/nypls-anne-carroll-moore-a-pioneer-who-opened-library-doors-to-kids.

Library of Congress. "Clarence Cameron White, 1880–1960." loc.gov/item/ihas.200038858.

Miller, Marilyn L., ed. "Mary Gould Davis." *Pioneers and Leaders in Library Services to Youth: A Biographical Dictionary.* Westport, CT: Libraries Unlimited, 2003.

Montreville, Doris de, and Elizabeth D. Crawford, eds. "Pura

Belpré." *Fourth Book of Junior Authors & Illustrators*.
H. W. Wilson: New York, 1978.

Morrison, Allen. "The Tramways of Ponce, Puerto Rico." Created June 10, 2010. tramz.com/pr/pc.html.

Nelson, Nicole. "NYPL's Ernestine Rose: Opening the Door to Diversity." *New York Public Library Blog*, March 15, 2021. nypl.org/blog/2021/03/15/nypls-ernestine-rose-opening-the-door-to-diversity.

New York Public Library Archives and Manuscripts. "Overview: Biographical/Historical Information." Clarence Cameron White Papers, 1901–1940. archives.nypl.org/scm/20793#bioghist.

NYPL Staff. "NYC Street Honors Pura Belpré, NYPL's First Puerto Rican Librarian." *New York Public Library Blog*, April 18, 2022. nypl.org/blog/2022/04/18/nyc-street-renaming-honors-pura-belpre.

"Pura Belpré Biographical Notes." Reforma: The National Association to Promote Library & Information Services to Latinos and the Spanish Speaking. reforma.org/content.asp?contentid=510.

Shulz, Dana. "Historic Map Shows the Manufacturing Industries of 1919 NYC." *6sqft Blog*, December 14, 2016. 6sqft.com/historic-map-shows-the-manufacturing-industries-of-1919-nyc.

MEG MEDINA is the eighth National Ambassador for Young People's Literature. She is a *New York Times* bestselling and award-winning author who writes for children and teens. She has won numerous awards for her work, including the Ezra Jack Keats Writer Award as well as the Pura Belpré Award and Honor. She is the 2019 Newbery Medal winner for her novel *Merci Suárez Changes Gears*. When she is not writing, she works on community projects that support Latino youth. She lives with her family in Richmond, Virginia.

Photo credit: Sonya Sones

You can visit Meg Medina online at
MegMedina.com
or follow her on Twitter
@Meg_Medina
and on Instagram
@MegMedinaBooks

MARILISA JIMÉNEZ GARCÍA is an associate professor of children's literature at Simmons University. She is the author of *Side by Side: US Empire, Puerto Rico, and the Roots of American Youth Literature and Culture*. She researches the role of youth literature in education and racial justice struggles in the US. Jiménez García's writing has appeared in the *Atlantic*, *Refinery 21*, *Children's Literature*, and *Latino Studies*.

You can follow Marilisa Jiménez García on Twitter @MarilisaJimenez

GILLIAN FLINT has worked as a professional illustrator since earning an animation and illustration degree in 2003. Her work has since been published in the UK, USA and Australia. In her spare time, Gillian enjoys reading, spending time with her family and puttering about in the garden on sunny days. She lives in the northwest of England.

Courtesy of the illustrator

You can visit Gillian Flint online at
gillianflint.com
or follow her on Instagram
@gillianflint_illustration

CHELSEA CLINTON is the author of the #1 *New York Times* bestseller *She Persisted: 13 American Women Who Changed the World*; *She Persisted Around the World: 13 Women Who Changed History*; *She Persisted in Sports: American Olympians Who Changed the Game*; *Don't Let Them Disappear: 12 Endangered Species Across the Globe*; *It's Your World: Get Informed, Get Inspired & Get Going!*; *Start Now!: You Can Make a Difference*; with Hillary Clinton, *Grandma's Gardens* and *Gutsy Women*; and, with Devi Sridhar, *Governing Global Health: Who Runs the World and Why?* She is also the Vice Chair of the Clinton Foundation, where she works on many initiatives, including those that help empower the next generation of leaders. She lives in New York City with her husband, Marc, their children and their dog, Soren.

Courtesy of the author

You can follow Chelsea Clinton on Twitter
@ChelseaClinton
or on Facebook at
facebook.com/chelseaclinton

ALEXANDRA BOIGER has illustrated nearly twenty picture books, including the She Persisted books by Chelsea Clinton; the popular Tallulah series by Marilyn Singer; and the Max and Marla books, which she also wrote. Originally from Munich, Germany, she now lives outside of San Francisco, California, with her husband, Andrea, daughter, Vanessa, and two cats, Luiso and Winter.

You can visit Alexandra Boiger online at
alexandraboiger.com
or follow her on Instagram
@alexandra_boiger

Read about more inspiring women in the

She Persisted series!